COPYRIGHT 1885 BY CURRIER & IVES, N.Y.

Bayou Foydras   St. Johns Ch.   Temple Sinai.   Lee Monument.   West End   1st. Presby Ch   Cotton Exchange.   Christ Church.   Bayou St. John   Congo Sq.   Spanish Fort   Opera House.   French Cathedral
St. Alphonsus Church.   (Lake Pontchartrain)   City Hall   Hotel Royal   Sugar Exchange.   Jackson Square
Qurch St. Mary's Assumption.   Annunciation Square.   St. Patricks Cathedral   Lafayette Square.   Jesuit Ch. and College   Pickwick Club.   Post Office and Custom Ho.   Depot Louisville & Nashville RR.   Sugar and Cotton Sheds   LEVEE.
                St. Charles Hotel   Canal St.   French M.

THE CITY OF NEW ORLEANS.

AND THE MISSISSIPPI RIVER.   LAKE PONTCHARTRAIN IN DISTANCE.

New Orleans

THEN AND NOW

New Orleans

THEN AND NOW

Sharon Keating

THUNDER BAY
P·R·E·S·S

San Diego, California

Thunder Bay Press
An imprint of the Baker & Taylor Publishing Group
10350 Barnes Canyon Road, San Diego, CA 92121
www.thunderbaybooks.com

Produced by Salamander Books,
an imprint of Anova Books Ltd.
10 Southcombe Street, London W14 0RA, UK

"Then and Now" is a registered trademark of Anova Books Ltd.

All notations of errors or omissions should be addressed to Thunder Bay Press,
Editorial Department, at the above address. All other correspondence (author
inquiries, permissions) concerning the content of this book should be addressed
to Salamander Books, 10 Southcombe Street, London W14 0RA, UK.

Library of Congress Cataloging-in-Publication Data available upon request.

1 2 3 4 5 14 13 12 11 10

Printed in China

AUTHOR ACKNOWLEDGMENTS
I would like to acknowledge my husband, Wayne, the New Orleans Public Library and the Historic
New Orleans Collection for their help with this book.

PICTURE CREDITS
The publisher wishes to thank the following for kindly supplying the photographs that appear in
this book:

"Then" photographs:
All "Then" images in the book were supplied courtesy of Library of Congress, except for the
following: Corbis (34, 42, 50, 52, 58, 68, 106, 110 inset, 112 inset, 132, 136, 142); New Orleans
Public Library (108, 112 main, 124, 126).

"Now" photographs:
All "Now" images were taken by David Watts, except for pages 113 and 115 (Anova Image Library).

Pages 1 and 2 show steamboats of the Mississippi, then (Corbis) and now (David Watts).

Endpapers show bird's-eye views of New Orleans: left, c. 1851 (Library of Congress), and right,
c. 1885 (Library of Congress).

Anova Books is committed to respecting the intellectual property rights of others. We have
therefore taken all reasonable efforts to ensure that the reproduction of all content on these
pages is done with the full consent of copyright owners. If you are aware of any unintentional
omissions, please contact the company directly so that any necessary corrections may be made
for future editions.

Introduction

The city of New Orleans occupies a singular place in the soul of the American nation. Born in a most inhospitable setting on the Mississippi River in the eighteenth century, it was sired by the French, mentored by the Spanish, and finally adopted by the United States. The River is the city's defining feature. Its location as a major port is its underlying raison d'être and helps explain its history as the most culturally diverse city in the South.

New Orleans has usually been portrayed as a primarily Southern city. However, it is apparent to anyone who visits that this city's location in the Deep South has informed, but not dominated, its culture. The Europeans who settled here became known as Creoles, along with the generations following. The remnants of the French and Spanish legacies are deeply ingrained in the language and customs. Thus, there are banquettes instead of sidewalks, and many buy produce at the French Market. Most of Spain's legacy is visible in the architecture of the French Quarter, or as is known by its French name, the Vieux Carré, as the Spanish rebuilt much of this section after several fires destroyed the earlier buildings. The Louisiana State Museum is in the Cabildo, and was originally built by the Spanish to serve as the capitol.

The rich fusion of traditions is not confined to those earlier settlers. African slaves, a number of whom were able to buy their freedom, contributed their lush heritage to the mélange. Haitians fleeing after the slave revolts in that country also became *les gens de couleur libres*, free persons of color, and their descendants were also Creoles, sometimes called Creoles of Color. Native Americans developed relationships and intermingled with both the Europeans and the people of color. All of these groups combined resulted in a population unlike any other, even unique within the state of Louisiana itself.

When it was purchased by the United States, Louisiana—and New Orleans in particular—truly appeared to be a foreign country. Unlike the rest of the nation, it was predominantly Catholic and the major language was still French. Customs ordinary to New Orleans, such as quadroon balls and the practices of voodoo religion, were exotic. Due to its location as a large port, immigrants from all over the world have settled there, and Italian, Irish, German, and many other peoples have added spice to what has become the sound and flavor of the city.

For a while, the culture clash with the Americans became too much for the Creoles, and different sectors of the city were formed. The Garden District became home to the rich Americans while the Creoles continued to live on the other side of Canal Street. The only mingling between them was for the necessary evil of doing business. Today, the streets on the Creole side of Canal have maintained their French names, such as Chartres and Decatur, while on the other side, those same streets have "American" names such as Camp and Magazine.

New Orleans is a Southern city, too. But it is not only moonlight and magnolias, sweet tea or mint juleps, although you can find all of that there. It is not only Bourbon Street or Frenchman Street, although they still remain primary tourist destinations with many great bars and restaurants. It is also a place of history, full of trials and tribulations. During the Civil War, "the Queen of the South" and its position as a river port was a prime target for the Union army. Under Union occupation, New Orleans never bowed its head, but chose to snub the invading Yankees rather than recognize them. It may have been conquered, but it was never subdued. The image of Benjamin "Spoons" Butler adorned the bottom of many a lady's chamber pot.

This has always been a place of contrast. In its career, New Orleans has been home to wealthy Creoles, has quartered bayou pirates, has given refuge to riverboat gamblers, and has housed sugar barons. At least one voodoo queen is buried in a Catholic cemetery, and most New Orleanians do not find this strange. It is accepted fact that there would be no Mardi Gras for the sinners if there were no Lent for the saints, so the one necessarily makes room for the other. The city has openly honored its religious and treasured its luminaries, while by the same token, it has acknowledged its villains and scoundrels.

From the Caribbean through the port came the devastating yellow fever in the nineteenth and early twentieth centuries. The once proud Pontalba buildings had become slums for the newly arrived immigrants, and a breeding ground for the epidemic. The subtropical climate allowed the virus to flourish, decimating the population. Those who could afford to leave did so during the summer months. Eventually, drainage was improved, helping to quell more epidemics. The Pontalba buildings are once again choice real estate in the French Quarter.

New Orleans has been harassed by hurricanes, flooded, and nearly destroyed by the levee failures. In the aftermath of Hurricane Katrina, the general spirit of the city was shaken but, as a whole, it was never broken. It didn't occur to most New Orleanians that there should be no Mardi Gras or Jazz Fest. The motto continued to be *Laissez les bon temps rouler*, or "let the good times roll." Then, more than ever, the city chose to celebrate life even as it mourned its losses.

Today, it is being lovingly rebuilt by humanitarians from all over the world, some of whom are adding their own zest and expanding the culture yet again. For this, the city is profoundly grateful. Her landscape may be evolving but her essence remains the same—and the music and food are like nowhere else on the planet. There are now more places to eat than before Hurricane Katrina. Outdoor concerts and sidewalk musicians abound. Music is everywhere, good music whatever your taste may be. The pictures change but the traditions remain as always, spiritual and earthly, pious and profane, troubled yet joyous.

Welcome to New Orleans.

JACKSON MONUMENT
AND ST. LOUIS CATHEDRAL

The square at the heart of New Orleans

Left: This beautiful square has always been a public space since the founding of New Orleans. Jean-Baptiste Le Moyne, Sieur de Bienville, chose this spot at the head of one of the crescents of the Mississippi River to establish New Orleans in 1718. This square was the central element of a city plan laid out by Adrien de Pauger in 1721. Originally the Place d'Armes, it became the Plaza de Armas under Spanish rule, but the Creoles called it the Place Publique and the Americans called it the Public Square. It wasn't until 1851—when the statue of General Andrew Jackson, hero of the 1812 Battle of New Orleans, was erected—that it became Jackson Square. This photo is from 1902.

Above: The Baroness Micaela Almonester de Pontalba designed and built the two apartment buildings flanking the square and was responsible for refurbishing the square itself. Today the Pontalba Apartments are thought to be the oldest apartment buildings in the United States. Jackson Square remains the center of New Orleans. The city grew out and around it. Today it's a place where locals and tourists alike enjoy the artists, palm readers, street musicians, and entertainers that surround the square. The St. Louis Cathedral sits just outside of the square between the Cabildo and the Presbytère. In front of the square is a favorite place for tourists to begin a ride through the historic French Quarter on a horse-drawn carriage. Jackson Square is the site of the annual French Quarter Festival, held every April, an important part of which is the world's largest jazz brunch.

THE CABILDO

The seat of colonial power when the city was ruled by Spain

Left: The Cabildo, erected during Spanish rule, was used as the seat of administration for the entire province of Louisiana. It also housed both civil and criminal law courts. Spanish officials would use the second-floor balcony to view ceremonies, parades, and militia drills. This photo shows President William McKinley on the balcony in 1901, just months before he would be assassinated at the Pan-American Exposition in Buffalo, New York. The Cabildo was the site of the transfer of Louisiana from Spain to France in November 1803. Just twenty days later, France sold Louisiana along with considerably more land to the United States in the Louisiana Purchase. Dignitaries from the three nations officially met and concluded the transfer of land in this building.

Above: The Cabildo was turned over to the Louisiana State Museum in 1914 and is still in use as a museum today. It houses memorabilia from two centuries of New Orleans history and has been visited by five U.S. presidents. Most of the original structure had been destroyed in the Good Friday fire of 1794. It is separated from the St. Louis Cathedral by Pirate's Alley. According to legend, it was in this alley that Jean Lafitte and his privateers joined with the Americans to plan the British defeat in the Battle of New Orleans during the War of 1812. Also in this alley is the former small home of the great American author William Faulkner, which in now used as a bookstore.

PRESBYTÈRE

Gifted by the man who financed the Cabildo and the St. Louis Cathedral

Left: This photo shows the Presbytère, or "Priest House," in 1934. The Presbytère was built on the site of a former Capuchin monastery. Although it was intended to be used as a rectory, it never saw out that purpose. Construction began in 1791, and it was designed to match the Cabildo on the opposite side of the St. Louis Cathedral. Building was halted in 1798 when Don Andres Almonester y Roxas, who was paying for the work, died. In 1813 the second floor was finally added. The Presbytère was used as commercial space until 1834, when it became the home of the Louisiana Supreme Court. In 1847 the facade of the structure was changed with the addition of the mansard roof. The Presbytère was sold to the city in 1908 and to the State of Louisiana in 1911.

Above: Since the transfer of the Presbytère to the State of Louisiana in 1911, it has been used as a museum. Today it contains a large collection of Mardi Gras gowns and memorabilia in a much-visited exhibit. The alley between the cathedral and the Presbytère is named for one of the most beloved priests in New Orleans history, Pere Antoine. In 1970 the Presbytère was added to the National Register of Historic Places. The cupola was lost in a hurricane in 1915, but was eventually replaced in 2005. Photos of the St. Louis Cathedral and the two buildings flanking it—the Cabildo and the Presbytère—taken from Jackson Square are probably the most recognizable pictures of New Orleans. Don Andres Almonester y Roxas, the philanthropist who financed the Presbytère, the Cabildo, and the St. Louis Cathedral, is buried beneath the floor of the cathedral.

ORLEANS BALLROOM / BOURBON ORLEANS HOTEL

The building at 717 Orleans Street has been a school, a ballroom, and a hotel

Left: This photo, taken in 1953, shows one of the few remaining buildings in which the quadroon balls—where white gentlemen would rendezvous with the quadroon girls—were held. Quadroons were the offspring of white fathers and mixed mothers. Mixed-race dances became legal in 1799, and these ballrooms were the meeting places that often resulted in unique social arrangements that lasted many years. After a match was made, the gentleman would provide a home for the quadroon, and any children born of these unions were automatically free at birth. This large population of free people of color was unique to New Orleans in the 1800s. Often, to make additional money, the quadroons would set up boardinghouses in their homes for the many men who came into New Orleans on the river. In 1881 the Sisters of Holy Family established a school for young black and mixed-race girls in this building that lasted until the 1960s.

Above: Today New Orleans is known for many things, one of them being great cuisine. Much of New Orleans's reputation for gourmet cooking can be traced to the competition among the quadroons to offer the finest meals to their boarders. Since the 1960s, the building at 717 Orleans Street, behind the St. Louis Cathedral Garden, has been used as a hotel. It currently houses the Bourbon Orleans Hotel, a beautifully restored European-style hotel offering suites with balconies overlooking Bourbon Street or the St. Louis Cathedral Garden. Orleans Street is much wider than most of the streets in the Vieux Carré as it emerges from the beautiful St. Louis Cathedral Garden.

ST. LOUIS HOTEL

Considered the grandest hotel outside of Paris, it once held slave auctions

Left: The St. Louis Exchange Hotel, which bore the name of the patron saint of New Orleans, was completed in 1838. It was considered to be the grandest hotel outside of Paris. The hotel had a rotunda that was sixty-six feet in diameter and paved with colored marble. It also had a copper-plated dome said to weigh 100 tons. The rotunda was used as an auction place for all commodities coming into the port of New Orleans, including slaves. In 1841 it was destroyed by fire, but rebuilt and later renamed Hotel Royal. The Americans, wishing to compete with the St. Louis Hotel, built the lavish St. Charles Hotel in the American sector of the city at about the same time. By the time Mark Twain visited in 1882, it had already been turned into "municipal offices." In 1906, when this photo was taken, the building had fallen into neglect and decay.

Above: When the St. Louis Hotel building was eventually torn down in 1915 after being partially destroyed by a hurricane, the incredible murals that covered the walls were purchased by France. Since 1960 the Royal Orleans Hotel, now the Omni Royal Orleans, has occupied this site on St. Louis Street between Royal and Chartres streets. The arches on the Chartres side of the hotel are from the old St. Louis Hotel and include a portion of the slave auction block originally located inside the rotunda.

NAPOLEON HOUSE

Still waiting for the scourge of Europe to escape from St. Helena

Left: The Napoleon House was constructed in 1794 and was owned by Claude Girod. Claude and his brother Nicholas conducted business on the first floor. Nicholas Girod, who became mayor of New Orleans, built the cupola on top so he could watch the Mississippi River for his ships coming into the port. The legend of this house is that when Napoleon was exiled, Mayor Girod planned to launch a rescue mission and build a refuge for Napoleon in this house should it succeed. This legend has never been proven as historically accurate, but it was sufficient to change the name of the house.

Above: The Napoleon House is considered to be one of the best surviving examples of French architecture in the Vieux Carré, favorably compared with the Ursuline Convent, and has been designated as a National Historic Landmark. The Impastato family has owned the Napoleon House since 1914 and operates the world-famous Napoleon House Bar on the first floor. The bar, named by *Esquire* magazine as one of the top 100 bars in America, plays classical music and serves food and beverages, but is most famous for the Pimm's Cup, a refreshing liqueur-based drink served on the rocks with a slice of cucumber. The Napoleon House offers typical New Orleans fare, such as jambalaya and gumbo, in one of the most historic settings in New Orleans.

OLD ABSINTHE HOUSE

A rare building that employs Spanish Colonial architecture, popular in Cuba

Left: The Old Absinthe House on the corner of Bourbon and Bienville streets in the French Quarter was built in 1806 by two Spanish traders as a home for their import business. It became a tavern shortly afterward. It is one of a handful of entresol buildings in New Orleans. Entresol buildings usually combined a retail establishment on the ground level, a residence on the top, and a hidden floor in between for the storage of goods. The building got its name in 1874 when a mixologist from Barcelona created a drink using absinthe, a narcotic-like spirit. Absinthe became illegal in 1912 and was replaced by Herbsaint in the mix. These photos are from 1902.

Above: In the late 1950s, the midfloor entresol was removed to create a higher ceiling for the first-floor bar. The building is now divided into three spaces. Two are used for restaurants; but there is still a bar located on the corner of Bourbon and Bienville, as it has been for the last 200 years. No visit to New Orleans is complete without a trip into the Old Absinthe House. Up until the 1960s the streetcar named Desire, made famous by Tennessee Williams in his play, ran down Bourbon Street and stopped at this corner. Today, the streetcar tracks are gone, but the atmosphere, history, and maybe even the odd ghost remain.

LaLAURIE MANSION

Events at the LaLaurie mansion once set the citizens of New Orleans into a raging mob

Left: This 1906 photo reveals none of the gruesome history of one of the most haunted houses in America. In 1832 Dr. Louis LaLaurie and his wife Delphine, wealthy Creole socialites who entertained on a grand scale, moved to their splendid quarters at 1140 Royal Street. Rumors of cruelty to slaves became horrifically real on April 10, 1834. On that night a fire broke out in the LaLaurie home, and when the volunteer firemen came to the scene, they discovered dozens of slaves chained to the wall in a secret attic. Some were in cages. Horrible mutilations had been perpetrated, and some slaves cried out, begging to be put out of their pain and misery.

Above: The LaLauries had already fled and were never found. However, a tombstone bearing Delphine's name was discovered nearby in St. Louis Cemetery No. 1, indicating that she died in 1842. Today the home has been restored to its original grandeur and is owned by the actor Nicolas Cage. The LaLaurie house has had many incarnations before being returned to its purpose as a residence. It was a saloon and a girl's school, a music conservatory, an apartment building, and a furniture store. Throughout its history, the LaLaurie mansion has brought grief to those who own it, and the reports of ghostly activity persist. Several people tell of seeing the ghost of a young slave girl jump to her death from the balcony outside of Delphine LaLaurie's room. A stroll past the LaLaurie house is a must for any visitor interested in the ghost stories that abound in New Orleans.

FRENCH OPERA HOUSE / INN ON BOURBON STREET

Where French-speaking Creoles enjoyed the grandest of art forms

Left: The beautiful French Opera House, as shown in this 1890 photo, was opened on December 1, 1859, on the corner of Bourbon and Toulouse streets. It was designed and built by architects James Gallier Jr. and Richard Esterbrook to seat 2,800 patrons, and was by all accounts a beautiful structure with excellent acoustics. Considering the total cost was $118,500 and that it was built in less than a year, the French Opera House was quite an achievement. It was especially designed for the presentation of grand opera and was perfectly suited for that purpose, though it ran for just two seasons before the Civil War put a temporary halt to the artistic program.

Above: The French Opera House was destroyed by fire in 1919 and never rebuilt. The building now located on the site is the Inn on Bourbon Street. While the architecture, when compared with the old French Opera House, leaves something to be desired, the inn is a comfortable place to stay and acknowledges its opera roots with the Café de L'Opera and the Puccini Bar. With the loss of the French Opera House, New Orleans not only lost its opera venue but also the traditional venue for Mardi Gras balls, debutante balls, and concerts. The New Orleans Opera Company has found a new home in the recently refurbished and state-of-the-art Mahalia Jackson Theater for the Performing Arts. There are now other venues for Mardi Gras balls, concerts, and benefits. But the French Opera House, which served as the center of social life in New Orleans for so many years, could never be replaced.

LaBRANCHE BUILDINGS

Some of the finest cast-iron galleries in New Orleans were an afterthought

This photo from 1925 shows only part of the complex of eleven Greek revival town houses built between 1835 and 1840 covering almost the entire block-bounded by St. Peter Street, Exchange Alley, Pirate's Alley, and Royal Street. The cast-iron lace gallery was an afterthought, added decades later. The whole complex is referred to as the LaBranche Buildings. Originally on this site was the residence of Francois Fleuriau, and part of the colonial prison yard. When Jean-Baptiste LaBranche purchased the property in 1835, there were several Creole cottages on the land, which made way for the new development. The cast-iron lacework on the balcony was commissioned by LaBranche's widow after his death.

Today this gallery of the LaBranche Buildings at Royal and St. Peter streets is one of the most photographed galleries in New Orleans. It's interesting to note that a gallery differs from a balcony in that a gallery has supports that go all the way to the ground, while a balcony does not. The combination of the lacy cast-iron railings of the gallery on the face of simple Greek Revival buildings is a remarkably beautiful sight. This is a fine example of how the Spanish left their mark on New Orleans architecture during their control of the city. These buildings are in use today as restaurant, commercial, and residential spaces. The buildings have been recognized as landmarks since 1961 by the Orleans Parish Landmarks Commission.

ROYAL STREET

New Orleans's prosperity was reflected in Royal Street, the street of banks

Left: This photo shows Royal Street as it appeared circa 1900. During the 1850s, New Orleans was the richest city in America and Royal Street was the street of banks. A walk down Royal Street is a walk through history. This storied street includes the residences of Francois Seignouret, a master carpenter who designed and manufactured furniture in his home. These "Seignourets" are prized by discriminating antique collectors. Prudent Mallard, another fine furniture maker, also lived on Royal Street. The Merieult House, now part of the Historic New Orleans Collection, was built in the 1790s, and is one of the oldest structures in the city.

Above: Today Royal Street runs from the edge of the French Quarter at Canal Street, goes through the French Quarter, and continues on through the historic streets of New Orleans. A stroll down Royal Street is a must for anyone interested in architecture. There are prime examples of early Creole architecture, Greek Revival houses with heavy wood cornices, and typical row houses of the 1830s. Many cast-iron balconies and galleries on the street are bedecked with hanging flowers and ferns. Toward Esplanade Avenue, Royal Street becomes residential and changes character as well. This more quiet part of Royal Street is in sharp contrast to the first few blocks that are filled with music, shoppers, and diners.

GAILLARD HOUSE

A traditional four-room Creole cottage

Left: This home, located on St. Ann Street in the French Quarter, was built in 1824 by Raimond Gaillard Jr., a free man of color. Under the Code Noir, a free person of color could own property and had many freedoms that were not normally granted to nonwhites in other parts of America during this time. Gaillard was a veteran of the Battle of New Orleans in the War of 1812 and built his home in the traditional Creole four-room cottage style that was popular at the time. The lines of the home are symmetrical, with doors opening into bedrooms. Kitchens were usually separate outbuildings to prevent fire from spreading. This photo shows the house in disrepair in 1930.

Above: The Gaillard house was restored in 1948 by Moise Goldstein. As this photo shows, the little cottage is still in use as a home. It sits in a quiet residential section of the French Quarter. This small Creole cottage is a fine example of the varied architecture of the French Quarter. While most visitors to the French Quarter think of the area as mostly commercial, this small home, typical of homes in the residential area, shows that the French Quarter is a real neighborhood. It just may be that New Orleans is the greenest city in America. Residents here have recycled old buildings for generations. Those buildings that are beyond repair are taken apart piece by piece, and components such as fireplace mantles, wooden floors, and cornices are reused to repair other old buildings or to add charm to new ones.

GARDETTE-LE PRETRE HOUSE

The building is also known as the "Sultan's Palace"

Left: In 1836 Joseph Gardette contracted with Frederic Roy to build this home on Dauphine Street. Gardette sold the home to Jean-Baptiste Le Pretre in 1839. It was Le Pretre who added the cast-iron galleries. During the Civil War in 1861, part of the captured flagstaff of Fort Sumter, sent to New Orleans by Confederate general P. G. T. Beauregard, was presented to the Orleans Guards in this house. However, the real draw of this house doesn't have anything to do with the Civil War. It relates to a legend about one of New Orleans's most famous ghosts. As the story goes, a mysterious Middle Easterner rented the mansion in the 1870s. The man and his harem were all found murdered, the result of a request by the angry sultan to whom the harem belonged. Since that time the home has been more popularly known as the "Sultan's Palace" or the "House of the Turk." This photo shows the house in 1935.

Right: Today the Sultan's Palace continues to be on the map of ghost hunters everywhere. It's now a private residence with the same graceful lacy galleries it sported in the nineteenth century. The house is on Dauphine Street in a quiet residential part of the French Quarter just a few blocks—yet worlds away—from the wild party atmosphere of Bourbon Street.

FIRST "SKYSCRAPER"

New Orleans's bid to rival Chicago barely got off the ground

The building in this 1935 photo is on the 600 block of Royal Street in the French Quarter, and is known as the first skyscraper built in New Orleans. At the time it was built, in the early nineteenth century, it was the tallest building in the French Quarter. Of course the term "skyscraper" hardly applies to this four-story building, and the word was not used in the nineteenth century. But when it was constructed, this building towered over every other building in the French Quarter. Its ironic title as the first skyscraper in New Orleans came in the twentieth century, when construction technology advanced enough to build a real skyscraper on New Orleans soil.

The building is still in use, but is certainly not considered tall. It had been trumped as the tallest building in New Orleans not least by the construction of the St. Christopher Hotel in 1893. Today the skyline of New Orleans reveals several true skyscrapers, the tallest of which is One Shell Square on the corner of St. Charles Avenue and Poydras Street. One Shell Square is fifty-one stories high. Height restrictions are strictly imposed in the Vieux Carré to maintain the historic nature of the area, making a view from a French Quarter street toward Canal Street a beautiful sight. The old buildings of the French Quarter juxtaposed against the tall, modern buildings of the Central Business District make a compelling contrast of one age against another.

BEAUREGARD-KEYES HOUSE

Escaping the wrecking ball in 1925, this house was lovingly restored by a novelist

Left: It is the occupants, as well as the architecture and history, that make this house famous. It was built in 1826 for a wealthy auctioneer by the architect François Correjolles. He was the son of refugees from the late eighteenth-century slave rebellion in the French colony of Saint-Domingue, now Haiti. Its Federal-style traits, such as the Tuscan columns with exterior stairways extending from either side, reflect growing Anglo-American influences at the time. Paul Morphy, the famous American chess player, was born in this house. Civil War general P. G. T. Beauregard lived in the house for a short time. This photo is from the turn of the twentieth century.

Above: The building was saved from demolition in 1925, but it was novelist Frances Parkinson Keyes who restored the house and the surrounding gardens after she took out a lease in 1944. She wrote several of her novels here, including *The Chess Players*, which featured the former resident of the house, Paul Morphy. Keyes also tells the story of the home's construction and history in that novel. Other novels written in this home include *Once on Esplanade*, *Blue Camellia*, *The River Road*, and *Crescent Carnival*. The Beauregard-Keyes House is no longer a private residence. It is open to the public and available for weddings and other special events. It is a fine example of a raised center hall house that is furnished in period pieces. The gardens are lush and set off the home beautifully. This house is on the National Register of Historic Places.

URSULINE CONVENT

One of the oldest buildings in New Orleans, but no longer home to nuns

This photo of the Ursuline Convent was taken in 1910. Home to the Ursuline nuns who arrived in New Orleans in 1727, this is one of the two oldest buildings in New Orleans. The Ursulines came to New Orleans to educate those who most needed education and were unlikely to get it from the French and Spanish in the early eighteenth century—mostly girls and Native Americans. The present building is from 1752 and survived two devastating fires that destroyed most of the old city in 1766 and 1788. It was in this building that the nuns prayed to Our Lady of Prompt Succor to save the city in times of disaster, such as during wars and hurricanes. The building also housed the residence of the archbishop and served as a meeting place for the Louisiana legislature.

It no longer serves as a home for the Ursulines, who moved to new quarters uptown in 1824. The Ursuline nuns continue to educate girls in New Orleans in the oldest school for girls in the United States. The old convent building still maintains a beautiful formal garden, and behind the main building there is a peaceful walled courtyard. In the main building is the original handcrafted cypress staircase that the Ursuline nuns climbed for so many years. The convent now functions as an archive for the Archdiocese of New Orleans, with documents dating back to 1718. The main lodge is filled with dozens of oil paintings, statues, and bronze busts. Smaller rooms recall the former convent's many functions over the years. The buildings were restored and repaired in the 1970s.

FRENCH MARKET

Nowhere was the city's diverse background more apparent than in the French Market

Left: Everyone in the family came to the French Market in 1910, as this photo shows. If the Vieux Carré is the heart of New Orleans, then the French Market is the heart of the Vieux Carré. The market served as a grocery store and meeting place to swap recipes and the news of the day. New Orleans's location on the Mississippi River made it easy for merchants and farmers to get their products to the market. The vendors and their wares were varied. Free people of color sold coffee, the French sold meat, the Spanish and Italians sold fruit, and Germans sold vegetables. There were Moors, with their strings of beads and crosses fresh from the Holy Land. Jews, Chinese, Irish, and Creoles—all met at the French Market.

Above: As shopping for fresh produce dwindled in the twentieth century, so the market contracted back to the main buildings, leaving this far end redundant, eventually being replaced by a traffic median. The market buildings were completely renovated recently and a flea market has been added, making the French Market several blocks long. A statute of Joan of Arc, patron of New Orleans, has been placed in front of the market in a small square. To add interest, through the year there are a series of events including the Creole Tomato Festival, Boo Carré Halloween and Harvest Festival, and a Christmas tree lighting ceremony.

FRENCH MARKET

Historians believe there was a market on this site before there was even a settlement

Left: The French Market has existed on this site since 1791, and it has changed and expanded over time. This photo, taken around 1900, shows the bustle surrounding the market that still occurs today. In the late nineteenth century, many of the vendors were Sicilian, immigrants originally recruited by plantation agents in the 1880s and 1890s as migrant farmworkers to compete with the labor of the freedmen. This market predates New Orleans, as it was used as a trading spot by the Louisiana Choctaws living in the area before the eighteenth century. The French Market is where New Orleanians have come to buy fresh food for over 200 years and is America's oldest public market.

Above: The French Market on Decatur Street has survived several changes of nationality, from when Louisiana reverted from French to Spanish rule, to when it went back to French control, and to its sale to the United States in 1803. Thomas Jefferson considered New Orleans the crown jewel in the territory obtained in the Louisiana Purchase. It now sits at the center of the historic French Market district, making up six blocks and consisting of the Butcher's Market, the Cuisine Market (occupying the old Seafood Market), the Bazaar Market, the Red Stores, the Vegetable Market, and the Farmers' Market Sheds—one of which is used by farmers to sell produce direct to the consumer while the other houses the flea market.

CAFÉ DU MONDE

Serving coffee and beignets since 1862

Left: This photograph shows Café du Monde in the heat of a summer night around 1920. The café is the original French Market coffee stand, established in 1862 at one end of the Halle des Boucheries, or Butcher's Market, and it is the building's oldest tenant. The original market was destroyed in a hurricane in 1812, and the building that exists today was constructed the following year. Around the time of the Civil War and the federal occupation, chicory began to be added to coffee served at the café, a tradition that has lasted 150 years.

Above: Café du Monde has been owned and operated by the Fernandez family since 1942. It is still a favorite for natives and visitors alike, who can enjoy strong chicory coffee and beignets. Over time, the café has expanded outward with tables overlooking Jackson Square and Decatur Street. Generations of New Orleans children and adults have long enjoyed sugary beignets at any time of the day. It is open 24/7 except on Christmas Day and when the occasional hurricane strikes.

MADAME BEGUE'S / TUJAGUE'S

The restaurant that became a New Orleans institution by serving one meal a day

Left: In 1906 this small corner restaurant was Madame Begue's. Since the 1860s, Elizabeth Kettenring Dutrey Begue, known as Madame Begue, fed the people of the French Quarter—especially those out to shop at the French Market—from her restaurant on the corner of Madison and Decatur. The original name of the restaurant was Dutrey's. When her husband—who was a butcher by trade—died, she married Hippolyte Begue and changed the name of the restaurant to Begue's. She served only one meal, a large breakfast at 11:00 a.m. That was a perfect time for dockworkers who had been on the job since early morning. In 1884 these elaborate late breakfasts with champagne were discovered by tourists who came to New Orleans for the World's Fair. Thus, the champagne brunch, a New Orleans tradition, was born.

Above: Madame Begue died in 1902 and the restaurant was taken over by her daughter and son-in-law. This corner is now occupied by Tujague's, a restaurant with its own storied history. Guillaume Tujague was a butcher in the French Market for three years before he established Tujague's Restaurant in 1856, a few doors down from Madame Begue's. Madame Begue's was his biggest competition. Eventually, the owners of Tujague's and Begue's joined forces and hung up the Tujague sign on the Begue corner in 1914. However, Madame Begue has not been forgotten. The Royal Sonesta Hotel has a restaurant named Begue's that serves a champagne brunch in her honor. The champagne brunch is also available in many other fine New Orleans restaurants and is a favorite way to celebrate holidays.

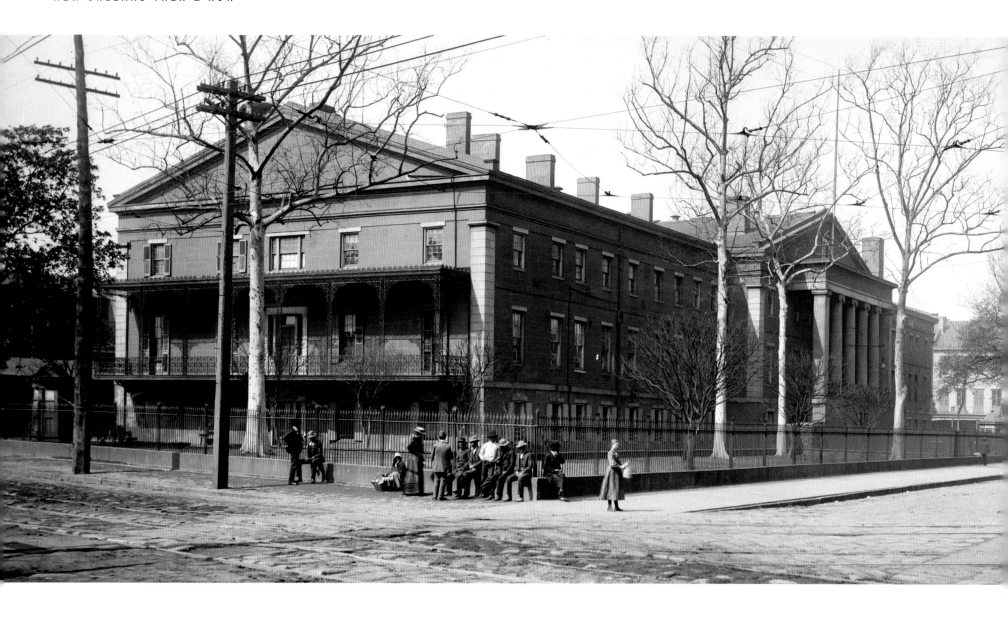

U.S. MINT

An important resource for the Confederacy that was lost in the 1862 seizure

This 1880 photo shows the neoclassical structure built in 1835 by the U.S. government to mint coins. At its peak in the 1850s, the mint produced about $5 million in gold and silver coins per year. When Louisiana seceded from the Union before the Civil War, the mint was seized and then turned over to the Confederates, who used it to mint their currency and to house troops. The U.S. government regained control of the mint after New Orleans was seized in 1862. The new governor of the city, Major General Benjamin Butler, provoked strong criticism by executing William B. Mumford, who had torn down a flag that victorious commander David G. Farragut had placed on the U.S. Mint. It was used once again to mint U.S. currency, thus took its place in history as the only mint to produce currency for both sides during the conflict.

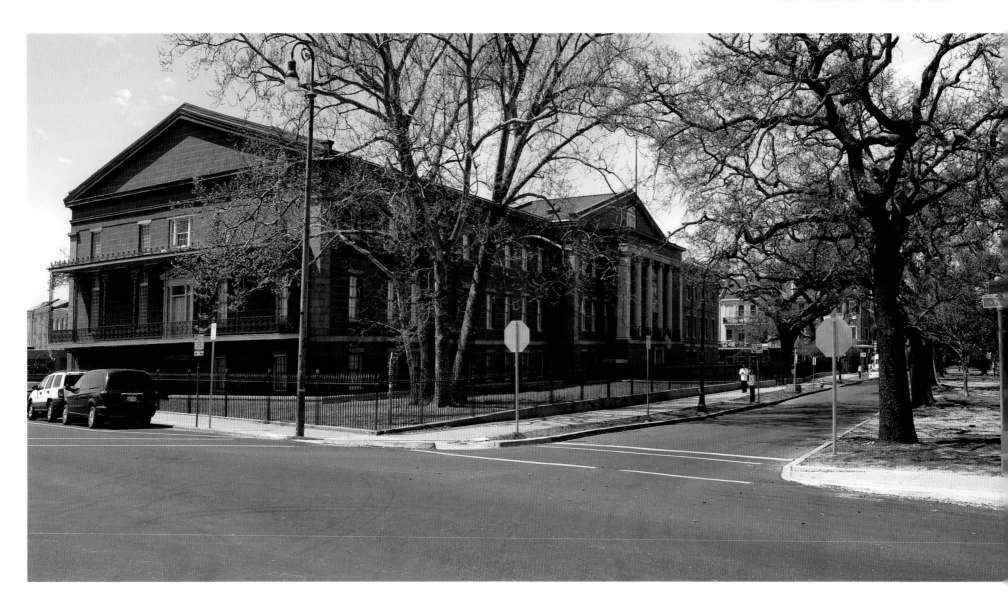

It ceased operations as a mint in 1909. Since that time the building has been used for various purposes by the federal government, including a prison for bootleggers during Prohibition. It was turned over to the State of Louisiana in 1966 for use as a museum. The New Orleans Mint now features a world-famous exhibit on jazz. The third-floor auditorium and wide, covered balconies look out over the historic French Market and French Quarter, and the lighted cityscape of the Central Business District. Many festivals, including the French Quarter Festival and the Creole Tomato Festival, are held on the grounds of this grand old building. It is on the National Register of Historic Places and is one of the many museums in the French Quarter under the umbrella of the Louisiana State Museum system.

SUPREME COURT BUILDING

Considered a monstrosity when it was first imposed on the French Quarter

Left: This 1910 photo, taken shortly after the building was completed, shows what is perhaps the most controversial structure in the French Quarter. Built in 1910 as the "new courthouse," the plan had been to tear down slums and replace the Cabildo and the Presbytère with a new home for the judicial system of New Orleans. Unfortunately, the so-called slums torn down on the site of the new courthouse were nineteenth-century Creole houses that were in disrepair, yet still historically significant. The new courthouse, a huge Beaux-Arts building, was considered by many to be a monstrosity, completely out of scale with the area.

Above: The courthouse was abandoned in 1958 when the courts moved to a new location. The State Agency of Wildlife and Fisheries took over the building for some time. When that agency moved out, the building went into disrepair. After years as home to the Louisiana Wildlife and Fisheries in New Orleans, the courthouse has been restored to its former glory and again houses the Louisiana Supreme Court and the Fourth Circuit Court of Appeal for Louisiana. A statue of Edward Douglass White, the only United States Supreme Court justice from Louisiana, who served from 1910 to 1921, stands in front of the building. It is now an accepted part of the French Quarter, and the verdant lawns and landscaping around the building have helped to soften the size of the large structure. The interior marble floors and stairs make for an elegant space that also houses the Louisiana Law Library and the Louisiana attorney general's office.

Above: On August 29, 2005, the levees broke after the eye of Hurricane Katrina passed near New Orleans. Over 80 percent of the city flooded as a result, causing perhaps the worst natural disaster in American history. Only the oldest part of the city and, ironically, areas closest to the river, escaped the devastation. This photo shows the flooding on Canal Street from Claiborne Avenue looking toward the Mississippi River shortly after the levee failure. The floodwaters remained for several weeks, causing the entire city to be closed down. The higher ground closer to the Mississippi River, including the French Quarter, remained dry. Some of New Orleans is below sea level, but the oldest parts of the city and those parts nearest the river and Lake Pontchartrain are above sea level.

CANAL STREET

The central artery of the city marking the boundary between districts

Right: Although New Orleans still has more recovery to complete, the downtown, uptown, and French Quarter sections of New Orleans are functional again. Visitors to the city will enjoy the same hotels, tourist attractions, and even more restaurants than before Hurricane Katrina. Some areas remain to be redeveloped, and New Orleans has conducted an extensive program to plan for the future.

TULANE UNIVERSITY MEDICAL CENTER

Many medical facilities have been restored post-Katrina, while others still await their fate

Left: The Tulane Medical School was founded in 1834 and is the second-oldest medical school in the South. Tulane has since become one of the nation's most recognized centers for medical education. Tulane has three primary locations in New Orleans. The one pictured here is on Tulane Avenue, across from the Tulane Teaching Hospital. In 2005, during the aftermath of the levee failures, most of New Orleans's hospitals were flooded and seriously damaged. Only two of the city's many hospitals avoided the devastating floodwaters—the Children's Hospital and the Touro Infirmary. With so little health care available after Katrina, a temporary emergency hospital was set up in the former Lord & Taylor department store on Poydras Street.

Above: The floodwaters are gone and some hospitals have been restored. Thankfully, that includes the Tulane Medical Center. However, health care remains a problem in New Orleans with the loss of so many medical professionals and facilities. Perhaps the most devastating loss was the Charity Hospital, part of two teaching hospitals associated with the Louisiana State University Medical Center. The Art Deco building, part of the New Orleans skyline since 1939, remains closed since Hurricane Katrina. Plans to build a new hospital in Mid-City are still controversial, and there is a strong movement to restore the existing Charity Hospital. The impetus is toward building a new medical care and research corridor in this area.

CUSTOM HOUSE / AUDUBON INSECTARIUM

The size of the Custom House was a reflection of New Orleans's importance as a port

Left: New Orleans's location on the Mississippi River made the city one of the major ports of the United States, and a large customs house was needed. The U.S. Custom House on Canal Street was begun in 1848 but not fully completed until after the Civil War. This building, which also served as a post office and housed other federal offices, was one of the largest buildings in New Orleans at the time it was built. It takes up an entire city block and is basically a Greek Revival design with Egyptian Revival accents. The photo shows the building in 1901.

Above: The grand Marble Hall in the center of the building is one of the finest Greek Revival interiors in the United States. The building was used as an office by Major General Benjamin "Spoons" Butler, the officer in charge of New Orleans during Union occupation, and also served as a prison for Confederate soldiers. The U.S. Custom House is in use today for a vastly different purpose. It is operated by the Audubon Institute as the Audubon Insectarium. It is the largest museum in North America devoted to insects and their relatives, and houses thousands of live and preserved specimens. Since its opening in 2005, it has become a favorite place for families to visit.

NEW
JACKSON
SQUARE
CIGARS

WINTER RACE MEETING
CRESCENT CITY JOCKEY CLUB, Races Start Nov. 100 Days

LEON FELLMAN

016321. CARONDELET STREET, NEW ORLEANS, LA.

CARONDELET STREET

Still a thriving area of commerce in the American Sector

Left: This photo, taken in 1906, shows the American Sector from Canal Street. Carondelet Street was a main commercial area at the turn of the century and remains so today. The streetcar is the St. Charles Avenue Streetcar that runs uptown from Canal Street. The width of Canal Street, compared with intersecting streets, is clearly seen here and is the result of the attempt by the Creoles to keep the Americans at a distance after the Louisiana Purchase in 1803. The architecture on the American side of the city is in sharp contrast to the architecture found on the other side of Canal Street, where the Creoles lived and worked together in the Vieux Carré.

Above: Canal Street remains one of the widest roadways in America that is not designated as an avenue or boulevard. This area was never residential; it was always mostly commercial and remains so now. Carondelet Street is a major part of the Central Business District, with many office buildings lining the sidewalks. Banks, restaurants, and hotels have been added to the landscape of Carondelet Street and the Central Business District, making this area busy not only during business hours but also at night. Although the buildings and the street have been modernized, one thing remains the same: the old green St. Charles Streetcar still runs down Carondelet Street to Canal Street and then goes back uptown on St. Charles Avenue.

MAISON BLANCHE / RITZ-CARLTON

The onetime home of Mr. Bingle

Canal Street was the main shopping street in New Orleans for generations, as shown in this photo from 1910. The building at 921 Canal Street was the home of the famed New Orleans department store Maison Blanche. The company was started by German émigré Isidore Newman in 1897, and its success helped spawn a chain of Maison Blanche stores. This particular building was erected between 1908 and 1909 (the inset shows its predecessor) and also housed commercial offices, as well as dentists' and doctors' offices. The department stores along Canal Street had large windows decorated with the latest fashions, and at Christmastime the front of this building was graced by the snowman Mr. Bingle, a favorite among New Orleanians.

The Maison Blanche Building is now part of the New Orleans
Ritz-Carlton Hotel. Most of the department stores along Canal Street
have been turned over to hotels, and as the tourism industry has
grown in New Orleans, the shopping on the street has declined. The
Ritz-Carlton suffered considerable damage in the aftermath of
Hurricane Katrina and the flooding necessitated a $106 million refit;
the hotel reopened for business in December 2006. Now Canal
Street, once filled with shoppers during the day and somewhat quiet
at night, is filled with tourists and locals both day and night. Mr.
Bingle has found a new home in City Park at the annual Celebration
in the Oaks light display.

ELKS PLACE

No longer a place where elks may safely roam—even as statues

Elks Place is actually a two-block stretch of the same street that is called Basin Street as you go downriver, or Loyola Avenue as you go upriver. In 1906, as this photo shows, Elks Place was a lovely area that included stately homes and a small park with a large statue of an elk at one end. The structure to the right of the elk statue and the pedestrians is the Old Elks Home, which was demolished in 1912 to make way for a new building. The photo shows a simpler life where everything from milk and eggs to fresh produce, cloth, and furniture was sold from horse-drawn carts. This area was also the medical center of the city with the imposing Eye, Ear, Nose, and Throat Hospital on the square; it was replaced by a new hospital and clinic in 1928.

Today, the area around Elks Place has lost all of its nineteenth-century charm and is in the middle of a bustling city. Gone are the beautiful old buildings and most of the green space. Many public buildings surround the area now as New Orleans has spread out from the Mississippi River toward Lake Pontchartrain. Elks Place is now at the edge of the Central Business District, but still in the hospital district of Tulane Avenue. The area is largely devoted to government buildings such as the public library. Also nearby are the New Orleans City Hall and the Louisiana State Office Building.

ALGIERS FERRY LANDING

Steam has been replaced by diesel, but the journey is still the same

Left: The Mississippi River is the reason New Orleans exists. The river was the main "highway" through America in the 1700s when New Orleans was founded. Algiers was part of the land grant given to New Orleans founder Jean-Baptiste Le Moyne, Sieur de Bienville, by the Company of the Indies in 1719. It became a thriving municipality on the west bank of the river and was absorbed into the city of New Orleans in 1870. A steam-driven ferry shuttled passengers and goods between the banks of the Mississippi in 1900, as shown in this photograph. In its heyday, Algiers had six ferries working to New Orleans's east bank, including one ferry capable of shuttling railroad cars and livestock.

Above: New Orleans still spans both banks of the Mississippi River, and the need for the Algiers ferry continues. The ferry is now driven by diesel engines and transports pedestrians and automobiles across the river every hour. The ferry ride is still free, but a trip across the nearby Crescent City Connection Bridge from Algiers to New Orleans will cost you $1.00. The ferry ride provides panoramic views of the skyline of New Orleans. On the Algiers side of the ferry you will find the Point, a neighborhood that still has the feel of a village with corner stores and neat houses with gingerbread trim.

RIVER CRESCENT

The river is still a driving force in the city's commerce

Left: New Orleans has been called the "Big Easy" for its relaxed attitude toward life and the "Crescent City" because it is nestled in a crescent of the Mississippi River. This photo, taken in 1910, shows the crescent looking downriver from the east bank with the tip of Algiers Point intruding just at right. Since its founding, New Orleans has been a large port city, and activity along the river has spread from the area in front of the Vieux Carré up and down both banks of the river. Living in a crescent-shaped city causes some confusion when giving directions. Except in the French Quarter where the streets are set in a grid pattern, going around the block doesn't always get you where you want to go when streets span out from a crescent.

Above: The Port of New Orleans is still one of the largest ports in the United States and, as shown in this photograph, wharfs extend well into the crescent of the Mississippi River. One sight that is always amusing to visitors is seen by standing on the east bank of the river in the French Quarter and looking at the smokestack of a refinery in Chalmette that appears to be directly across the river. But, because of the crescent, the smokestack is actually on the same east bank on which the visitor is standing. Because of this confusion, New Orleanians tend to give directions by references to the water rather than to the compass. The uptown river corner of a street means the corner that is on the river side, rather than the lake side, and the uptown side is in the direction of the upper part of the river.

VEE, FOOT OF CANAL ST., NEW ORLEANS.

LEVEE AT FOOT OF CANAL STREET

In the age of the steamboat, no place in New Orleans was more busy than the levee

Left: The levees were necessary in order for the French to build New Orleans. The Mississippi River was, and still is, unpredictable and has been known to jump its banks. The levee at the foot of Canal Street was a major site for river trade. It was the site of numerous warehouses and industrial wharfs, as well as floodwalls. This area remained basically utilitarian until the late 1980s. Wharfs for the loading and unloading of ships from all over the world were constructed on the river in front of the Vieux Carré and spread up and down the river. Cotton and sugar left from the ports and coffee and tropical fruit came in to be sent at first by steamboats and then by railroads around the country. This photo from around 1900 shows the levee as it looked when steamboats had the luxury of mooring side-on and didn't have to jostle for position.

Above: The levee has been reimagined as Woldenberg Park and is operated by the Audubon Institute. Named for philanthropist Malcolm Woldenberg, it is sixteen acres of green space in the French Quarter. Beginning at Canal Street and the Aquarium of the Americas, it continues down to the "Moonwalk" (named in honor of former mayor Maurice Edwin "Moon" Landrieu) across the street from Jackson Square. Woldenberg Park has several notable sculptures, including the city's Holocaust Memorial and the *Monument to the Immigrant*. This area is not used as it was a century ago. Now the area is home to steamboats docked and ready for a nostalgic trip on the mighty Mississippi River. It is no longer a place where dockworkers spend long, hard hours loading and unloading.

STEAMBOATS OF THE MISSISSIPPI

In the golden age of the steamboat, it would be hard to find a space to dock in New Orleans

Left: Steamboats served as the primary means of transportation on the Mississippi River since 1811. The *New Orleans* was the first steamboat, traveling from Pittsburgh to New Orleans on a harrowing journey that included surviving the New Madrid earthquake. The first regular routes were between New Orleans and Natchez, Mississippi, but within a few years, Louisville and St. Louis became important ports. Passenger travel by steamboat was common as well as comfortable, but these vessels often carried cargo. In 1870 the *Robert E. Lee* and the *Natchez* raced from New Orleans to St. Louis. The winner was the *Lee* with a time of three days eighteen hours fourteen minutes. The golden age of steamboats came to an end both with the advent of modern vessels with diesel engines, and railroads that supplanted cargo transportation.

Above: Steamboats are still in use, although only for passenger travel and tours. The calliope on the *Natchez* still serenades visitors to the French Quarter when it is docked. It is the ninth steamboat to bear the name. It was built in 1975 and is a real steamboat, although built to be much safer that its predecessors. Steamboat explosions were common in the nineteenth century—Mark Twain lost his brother Henry when the *Pennsylvania* exploded in 1858. Dinner cruises are popular with tourists as well as natives, but the boats will take longer cruises in the area, such as down to the Chalmette Battlefield, site of the famous Battle of New Orleans in the War of 1812. You can take a short voyage from the Aquarium of the Americas to the Audubon Zoo by way of the Mississippi River, or a long voyage down the river from states as far away as Iowa, to get a better idea of what life on the river was like. The fountain in the foreground is in the center of the Spanish Plaza. Given as a gift from Spain in 1976, the seating surrounding the fountain is decorated with the seals of the Spanish provinces.

POYDRAS STREET WHARF

Where ships unloaded a steady stream of coffee from Latin America

Left: In 1943 the Poydras Street Wharf was bustling with activity, as this photo shows. By the 1920s, this wharf was the central receiving point for the coffee industry. Coffee arrived in 130-pound bags that had to be carried by hand by the dockworkers. In the early twentieth century, the system was mechanized, replacing the need for much of the manual labor that had previously been employed along the river. Although coffee was the main import unloaded at this wharf, bananas and other tropical fruit from Latin America were typical cargoes at what was one of the major wharfs in New Orleans.

Above: Today, this area along the river is a pedestrian walkway outside of the Riverwalk Mall filled with shops and restaurants. There are several tiers that project out from the mall that provide places for viewing the activity on the river. Although New Orleans is still one of the largest ports in the United States, its expansion up and down the river from the original Vieux Carré has allowed more leisure access to the river, and offers great views and walks. Today, cruise ships rather than coffee boats are docked at the Poydras Street Wharf. The twin cantilever bridges—named the Crescent City Connection—were built in 1958 to connect the east and west banks of the Mississippi River.

SOUTHERN RAILWAY STATION

Located at the cultural crossroads of New Orleans, right next to Storyville

Left: The Southern Railway System Passenger Station was constructed in 1908 and demolished in 1956. This photo shows the station as it looked in 1910. When the station was built on the corner of Basin and Canal streets, it was at the cultural crossroads of New Orleans. The turning point for the old Basin Canal built by the Spanish in 1786 was nearby on Carondelet Street. The canal provided a link between the city and Lake Pontchartrain to the north. The railroad station was the terminus of the railroad where locals and visitors came and went. The area around the station was filled with lumberyards and mills. It was also adjacent to Storyville, home to legalized prostitution, dance halls, and great music venues featuring entertainers like Jelly Roll Morton and Louis Armstrong.

Above: Storyville is gone, and so is the original railroad station. Storyville was closed down by the U.S. military in the 1920s, and the dance halls and jazz joints that filled the area are also gone. The canal has been filled in and paved over with streets. But the area around Basin Street, known as Treme, is still home to many of New Orleans's fine musicians. This is the part of town that is home to many of the Native American tribes that parade at Mardi Gras and on St. Joseph's Day in a tradition that happens only in New Orleans. Part of the old structure has been restored and is now the Basin Street Station visitor and cultural center. The cultural aspect of the area remains intact with Armstrong Park, the Municipal Auditorium, and the beautifully restored Mahalia Jackson Theater.

MORTUARY CHAPEL / ST. JUDE'S

No longer caring for the souls of yellow fever victims

Left: The little chapel shown in this circa 1880 photo is the oldest existing church in New Orleans and is built on the edge of the Vieux Carré. It was called the Mortuary Chapel because bodies piled up to be buried during the deadly outbreaks of yellow fever. They would be brought here, outside of the city, until burial could take place. In the late nineteenth century it became a church for the city's Italian immigrants. This chapel is also the International Shrine to Saint Jude, the saint of the impossible. A plaque to the victims of yellow fever, dated 1826, stands next to the chapel. In the rear of the chapel stands the only extant statue of Saint Expedite. The story is that the statue arrived in a box marked "expedite," so the nuns gave the statue that name.

Above: St. Jude's is no longer the Mortuary Chapel, as the threat of yellow fever has long since passed. Now known as Our Lady of Guadalupe, it remains the International Shrine of Saint Jude. It is the official chapel of the New Orleans Police and Fire departments, which hold a celebratory mass there every year. The chapel sits on the edge of Treme, a neighborhood that is home to many fine New Orleans musicians. During the 1980s, many of the best New Orleans musicians, including Aaron Neville, Alan Toussaint, and Lady B. J., would sing at midnight mass here. A recording of one of those masses is highly prized among fans of New Orleans music.

ST. CHARLES AND CANAL

New Orleanians have been celebrating Mardi Gras since the eighteenth century

Above: The pageantry that is Mardi Gras is highlighted in this 1913 photo of the Rex Parade turning onto Canal Street from St. Charles Avenue. In 1913 some of the carnival parades continued across Canal Street and into the French Quarter. However, that practice was stopped in 1972 when floats got too large for the narrow streets. New Orleans has celebrated Mardi Gras in some form since the French first settled here in the early 1700s. Now the entire carnival season, from January 6, the Feast of the Epiphany (or King's Day) until Mardi Gras (Fat Tuesday), the day before Ash Wednesday, is cause for celebration.

Bottom right: Both St. Charles and Canal have been revitalized in recent years with upgrades to the sidewalks and landscaping. The city has also returned the Canal streetcar line to help with traffic and provide a fun, convenient way to travel up and down Canal Street, on the "neutral ground." However, for about two weeks before Mardi Gras, carnival parades roll down St. Charles Avenue onto Canal Street. These parades end on Fat Tuesday when Rex, King of the Carnival, and the rival Zulu parade (which started in 1909) roll through the streets of New Orleans. The party continues until midnight, when the streets are cleared and things go back to normal.

ST. CHARLES HOTEL

A grand rival to the St. Louis Hotel of the Vieux Carré

Left: The St. Charles Hotel is a prime example of the rivalry between the Creoles in the Vieux Carré and the Americans in the American Sector. In 1837 this grand hotel on "the Avenue" was built at a cost of $800,000 to rival the St. Louis Hotel in the Vieux Carré. Prior to the Civil War, much of New Orleans's social life revolved around events in these lavish hotels. Grand balls for Mardi Gras or debutantes were held in the lavish ballrooms of the St. Charles. This photo shows the grandeur of the hotel in 1900. The original building was destroyed by fire in 1851, and its replacement was erected shortly afterward. It was extensively renovated and expanded in 1878. At that point it had 400 rooms, office space, a restaurant, and a bar.

Above: The second St. Charles Hotel burned down in the early 1890s and was rebuilt in 1896. This third hotel was demolished in 1974. Since 1984, one of the tallest office buildings in New Orleans, the Place St. Charles, has stood on the site of the former St. Charles Hotel. The Place St. Charles is a fifty-three-story, 645-foot tall skyscraper in the Central Business District. Its architecture is vastly different to the hotel that formerly stood on this site. The new granite-and-glass structure is softened by the French Quarter–style balconies on the first three floors. It houses a hotel, a shopping mall, offices, and a food court. Although suitable for today's needs and an architecturally pleasing structure in its own right, the Place St. Charles could never replace the St. Charles Hotel and the era it represented.

ST. CHARLES AVENUE

The grand street of the American Sector

Left: By 1910 St. Charles Avenue had long been established as "the Avenue" of the American Sector, as this photo shows. Running uptown from Canal Street, St. Charles Avenue starts in the Central Business District, runs through the American Sector, past the Garden District, universities, and parks, and ends up in Carrolton at a bend in the Mississippi River. This view shows the beginning of St. Charles near its intersection at Canal Street. This part of St. Charles Avenue was largely commercial and was lined with office buildings, banks, and some shops, restaurants, and hotels. St. Charles Avenue widens at Lee Circle and has a large neutral ground in the middle to accommodate the St. Charles Streetcar line. The avenue at this point begins to become more stately, with mansions and large live oak trees lining the sides.

Above: St. Charles Avenue continues to be the main avenue on the American side of the city. The St. Charles Avenue Streetcar still runs on tracks in the middle of the street on the neutral ground for the entire length of the avenue and provides a scenic ride through uptown New Orleans for a nominal price. St. Charles Avenue is also the main route for Mardi Gras parades in New Orleans. The mansions along the avenue, built in the last century, are still occupied, and Audubon Park, established after the New Orleans World Cotton Centennial in 1884, gets more scenic every day with the live oak trees, palms, and abundance of birds. Tulane and Loyola universities front on St. Charles Avenue, and it is often called the "Avenue of Churches" for the many beautiful churches and cathedrals along the avenue.

COTTON EXCHANGE

When cotton was king, it required a building that was fit for one

Left: Cotton was king in New Orleans in the mid-nineteenth century, and the New Orleans Cotton Exchange Building was constructed to promote the cotton trade. The building housed the board of directors and members of various cotton committees that dealt with membership, information and statistics, trade, classification and quotations, finance, credits, and books relating to the cotton trade. Rules and regulations were written here, disputes were settled, and general information was disseminated in this building to all parties dealing in cotton. Mark Twain, visiting New Orleans in 1882, was impressed by what he saw: "When completed, the new Cotton Exchange will be a stately and beautiful building; massive, substantial, full or architectural graces; no shams or false pretenses of uglinesses about it anywhere. To the city, it will be worth many times its cost, for it will breed its species." This photo is from 1890.

Above: The replacement building of 1920 was designed by the architectural firm of Favrot and Livaudais; however, the trade was already on the wane compared to its nineteenth-century highs. Business dwindled and in 1962 the exchange closed. At its height, the Cotton Exchange occupied three buildings. The last of these structures remains standing on the corner of Carondelet and Gravier streets. Although it passed out of the hands of the exchange in 1962, it is still known as the Cotton Exchange Building. It now houses a boutique hotel, office space, and retail shops. While cotton is no longer king in Louisiana, it is still a major crop. Louisiana also grows sugar and New Orleans is the place where the process for the granulation of sugar was invented.

SCOTTISH RITE CATHEDRAL

Housing the oldest Valley of the Scottish Rite in the United States

Above: This building, constructed in 1850–53 and photographed in 1910, was originally home to the First United Methodist church of New Orleans. The plastered-brick Greek Revival church was a replacement for an earlier building that was destroyed by fire. That earlier building housed the first Methodist church in New Orleans. The New Orleans Scottish Rite Consistory purchased the property in 1902, as well as other surrounding buildings. The New Orleans Scottish Rite Consistory is the oldest valley in existence today. Over the next century, the consistory purchased more buildings and expanded its presence in New Orleans with a theater, a library, and the Scottish Rite Childhood Language Disorders Clinic.

Right: When the building was purchased in 1902, the consistory made changes to the facade, which are shown in this modern photo. The beautiful stained glass replaced the original front door, and later changes have enhanced the architecture of the building. The Scottish Rite Cathedral is on the National Register of Historic Places and is protected from any further renovations. The building is open to the public and contains an impressive library that not only contains the history of the consistory but also many extremely valuable and irreplaceable literary editions. A new addition was added in 1979, allowing the consistory to provide therapy rooms for its work with language disorders.

ORPHEUM THEATER

An intimate theater that suffered the tragedy of Katrina

Left: The charming, intimate neoclassic theater depicted in this circa 1930 photo was built in 1918 as a venue for vaudeville. The theater is an example of vertical hall theater construction, which was aimed at providing the best sight lines. Later a projector was added and the Orpheum became the RKO Orpheum, a movie theater seating about 1,800. It was a small, intimate theater with a large stage and deep orchestra pit. During the sad days of the Jim Crow laws, the first balcony was set aside for white patrons, and the upper balcony was for "Colored Only."

Above: In the 1980s the Orpheum underwent a complete restoration to become the home of the Louisiana Philharmonic Orchestra. Sadly, it was devastated by Hurricane Katrina. Floodwaters that filled the theater remained for weeks, ruining the lovely interior. The water level came up to cover all the stage and half the seats. All mechanical equipment in the basement was destroyed. The Philharmonic has moved to the newly renovated Mahalia Jackson Theater, and the Orpheum remains closed and dark. The faded marquee touting the final show set in the theater serves as a daily reminder of how much was lost and how much remains to be saved after Hurricane Katrina's floodwaters ravished the city. The much-needed restoration may begin soon, as the Orpheum has new owners.

MASONIC TEMPLE / HILTON HOTEL

A magnificent building lost to the wrecker's ball

This ecclesiastically themed building was designed by local architectural prodigy James Freret and built in 1891 for the Freemasons. It was one of the tallest buildings in the New Orleans Central Business District at that time. The Freemasons of the city came to Louisiana from France in 1791 and started their first lodge. The Freemasons kept records in French, the predominant language of New Orleans at the time. They remained deliberately inconspicuous until after the Louisiana Purchase in 1803, which brought them under the U.S. Constitution and gave them freedom of religion and assembly. The Freemasons used this monolithic neo-Gothic temple until 1926. This photo dates to 1910.

The building now installed at 333 St. Charles Avenue is quite different in architecture and use. The old 1891 building was replaced by this structure, which was originally called the Masonic Building. It is now the home of the Hilton Hotel and Luke, a restaurant owned by John Besh, one of New Orleans's premier chefs. Its location on the St. Charles Streetcar line in the Central Business District has kept the building in constant use since its construction. The building is perhaps more striking when it is viewed from across the street because it is surrounded by modern skyscrapers made of cement, glass, and steel.

LEE CIRCLE

General Robert E. Lee gazes north, some say for very good reason

Left: When the DeLord plantation was subdivided in 1806, the city surveyor, Barthelemy Lafon, envisioned a cultural center in the American Sector to compete with Jackson Square. He designed a large circle, Tivoli Circle, with a graceful waterway and a Greek Revival theme with streets named for the muses. This grand plan never materialized, but the circle was constructed. By 1845 the area had deteriorated, and during the Civil War the area became a camp for Yankee soldiers. After the war, the circle became an area for traveling circuses to set up stalls. When General Robert E. Lee died in 1870, it was decided that a statue would be erected in his honor. The monument was dedicated in 1884 and the circle was renamed Lee Circle. General Lee stands proud in this 1906 photograph.

Right: Lee Circle is a well-known landmark in New Orleans today. It is said that General Lee was placed on the monument facing north, because it would never be a good idea to turn your back on a Yankee. While Lafon's dream of the ideal city in the Greek style did not come to pass, the streets near the Lee monument still retain their muse names and sport many grand homes. The area surrounding Lee Circle has now become a museum and art district. The National World War II Museum, the Ogden Museum of Southern Art, the Contemporary Art Center, and the Confederate Museum are all within two blocks of the circle. During Mardi Gras, the area around the monument is filled with viewing stands so people can watch the passing parades.

HOWARD LIBRARY / CONFEDERATE MUSEUM

A fascinating museum set within an architectural museum piece

Above: This building dates back to 1891 and contains one of the largest collections of Confederate memorabilia in the world. The museum owes much of its collection to Frank Howard, a New Orleans philanthropist who constructed this building for use as a public library in honor of his father, Charles T. Howard. The architect was H. H. Richardson, the New Orleans architect responsible for the building style known as Richardson Romanesque. It has changed little since its construction, as can be seen when this circa 1900 photo is compared to the modern photo. When the library outgrew these quarters in the 1940s, it moved to Tulane University.

Right: This architectural gem is now known as the Louisiana Confederate Museum and is operated by a nonprofit group with the mission of preserving the history and artifacts in the museum. This museum is the second-largest Confederate museum in the country and contains letters and artifacts from Jefferson Davis, the president of the Confederacy, as well as many other Civil War–era exhibits. The museum has been a draw for the establishment of other nearby museums, including the Contemporary Art Center, the Ogden Museum of Southern Art, and the National World War II Museum, which can be seen at right and for which local author Stephen Ambrose (Band of Brothers, D-Day) was a great supporter.

CONFEDERATE MEMORIAL HALL

A treasure trove for those seeking out Confederate battle flags

Left: This building is an adjunct to the Louisiana Confederate Museum and was built in the complementary Richardson Romanesque style. The photo was taken in 1906. The ownership of the building has been contested for years. When Frank Howard commissioned the building next door as a library in honor of his father, he supposedly gave this adjacent building to the Louisiana Historical Society for use as a Confederate museum. However, the language of that donation has been the source of debate. The problem was exacerbated after Tulane University, which inherited ownership of the adjoining Howard Library, sold the property to the University of New Orleans.

Above: Now known as Confederate Memorial Hall and nicknamed "the Battle Abbey of the South," the museum is an adjunct of the Howard Confederate Museum (visible at left). The museum has over 125 battle flags of the South and a large collection of Confederate uniforms, guns, and swords, including the formal presentation sword of General P. G. T. Beauregard. Also contained in the museum are over 500 rare photographs in several media and a fine collection of art by Southern artists. The museum also has a collection of artillery used in the Civil War, including the cannon that sits proudly in front of the building.

ST. PATRICK'S CHURCH

Serving the Irish immigrant community since 1840

St. Patrick's Church, shown here in the late 1950s, dates back to 1840, although the parish of St. Patrick's was established as early as 1833. St. Patrick's overlooks Lafayette Square in the American Sector of the city. During the 1830s and 1840s, services were held only in French in New Orleans. Masses at the St. Louis Cathedral on Jackson Square were mostly reserved for the Creoles. Irish Catholic immigrants to New Orleans were forced to crowd into a few pews in the rear of the church. A decision was made to build a grand church in the American Sector, where services could be heard in English and the Irish could sit in the front, middle, or rear pews as they chose. St. Patrick's is the cornerstone of the American Sector's answer to Jackson Square.

The grand church is now on the National Register of Historic Places and is still an active parish. James Gallier, the famed Irish architect, accomplished a remarkable feat of engineering skill when he was called in to repair the original foundation soon after the church was built. Fortunately, Gallier happened to be a member of the parish. The beautiful old church was heavily damaged in 1965 during Hurricane Betsy, but has been completely restored. Today it stands in what is known as the Warehouse/Arts District in the American Sector. The congregation comes from far and wide to attend Mass at St. Patrick's. Another example of Gallier's beautiful architecture, Gallier Hall, is just across Lafayette Square.

MARGARET MONUMENT

The statue cost $6,000, but only nickels and dimes were accepted to pay for it

This 1906 photo shows the monument to Margaret Haughery (1813–82) created in 1884, honoring a great philanthropist whose death sent the city into mourning. There is some debate as to whether this is the first or second statue erected for a woman other than a muse or goddess in the United States. Haughery was an Irish immigrant who, after the death of her husband and child, devoted herself to the betterment of women and children. She opened a dairy and delivered milk, and later distributed bread from her own bakery among the poor. She opened orphanages, nursed sick and dying women, and was called the "Angel of the Delta" for her role in caring for the women and children of New Orleans during the Civil War while the men were away.

The area where the statue remains is known as Margaret Park. Margaret Haughery is still in her place of honor on Camp Street, although the neighborhood has changed somewhat. The Lower Garden District is a mix of grand homes and shotgun doubles. St. Teresa's Church, which Haughery funded and helped build, is still in use. Nearby Coliseum Square is a lovely little park. In the next block are interstate highway underpasses. The Orphan Asylum in the background of the old photo is now a guest house. The statue of Margaret Haughery shows her as she was in life, wearing a simple dress with a knitted shawl, caring for a child.

ST. SIMEON'S SELECT SCHOOL

The school on Annunciation Street has long since disappeared

Left: The building on Annunciation Street occupied by St. Simeon's Select School was originally constructed in 1834 as the private mansion for the Saulet family. Subsequently, it became a private Catholic school. This photo, taken in 1906, shows some of the schoolchildren at play. During this time, the school, standing about three blocks from the Mississippi River, was probably a great place for children to enjoy cool river breezes while playing or learning.

Above: In 1922 St. Simeon's became St. Luke's Private Sanitarium. Not long afterward, Mercy Hospital purchased the building and remained there until it was demolished in 1959. Nothing was built on the site, which is now adjacent to the staging area for the New Orleans Convention Center. A large apartment building near the site is named after the Saulet family. The tradition of private Catholic education has remained strong in the New Orleans educational system. That can be traced back to the attitudes of the French and the Spanish, who founded the city, that education is far too important to be left up to the state. Before Hurricane Katrina, over 40 percent of New Orleans children were educated in Catholic schools.

ESPLANADE AVENUE

A grand old residential district on the route out to City Park

Left: In the early days of New Orleans this area, at the downriver end of the Vieux Carré, was often fortified against possible enemies that might invade the city by sailing up the Mississippi River. From 1742 to 1792, the site that would later become the head of Esplanade Avenue was part of the Marigny plantation. It became property of the city in 1810 and was subdivided into lots. Artisans and tradesmen, many of them free people of color, built homes on the lots. When the city became more affluent in 1835, Esplanade Avenue was paved, and streetlamps and banquettes (sidewalks) were installed. By the time this photo was taken in 1900, larger, more lavish homes were built here.

Above: Esplanade Avenue is now the border between the Vieux Carré and the neighborhood of Faubourg Marigny. The street has a wide variety of architectural styles, with the larger, more luxurious homes built after the upgrades on the street. Esplanade Avenue is still largely residential and runs out to the entrance of City Park and the New Orleans Museum of Art. The avenue passes through the Esplanade Ridge neighborhood of New Orleans, so named because it is located on a higher strip of land that marks the old Native American portage connecting Bayou St. John with the river. This neighborhood suffered from the 1960s construction of Interstate 10, which split the neighborhood.

CITY HALL / GALLIER HALL

A place of reverence for supporters of the South; Jefferson Davis lay in state here

Left: This 1910 photo shows the old city hall that was built between 1845 and 1853, and which served as the seat of government until the 1950s, when it was moved to a new building on Poydras Street in the Central Business District. When it was built, the Creole French did not welcome the Americans, and New Orleans was divided into three municipalities. This Greek Revival building was originally headquarters for the Second Municipality, and ultimately became New Orleans City Hall. It is also called Gallier Hall in honor of its renowned architect, James Gallier Sr.

Above: No longer referred to as City Hall, Gallier Hall has seen many historic events since its construction. It was the site of numerous major events over the years. Jefferson Davis and General P. G. T. Beauregard, and even Ernie K-Doe, a New Orleans music legend, lay in state here. It is the place where Rex toasts the mayor on Mardi Gras Day, and its elegant setting is the site of many major political and private functions. Across the street is Lafayette Square, a green space in the Central Business District. The statue of philanthropist John McDonough, who divided his fortune between New Orleans and Philadelphia for the construction of public schools, can be seen in both photos.

HENRY CLAY STATUE, CANAL STREET

The statue is gone and the canal, for which the street was named, never arrived

Left: Canal Street was so named because it was originally intended that a canal be dug along the street. That never happened, but the name stayed. Canal Street is the border between the Creole section and the American Sector. The city leaders decided to beautify Canal Street in the 1850s, and a circle at the intersection of Canal Street and St. Charles Avenue was created. In 1856 a statue of Henry Clay, a statesman admired by the leaders of the city, was placed in the center of that circle. In this photo, taken circa 1890, the statue looks down Canal Street toward the Mississippi River. Other plans to add more monuments to Canal Street never came about, so Clay stands alone.

Above: Both the circle and the statue are now gone. Streetcars run along the neutral ground and Canal Street has been widened to facilitate the flow of traffic. Clay's statue was moved from its place on Canal Street in 1900. It now watches over the comings and goings in Lafayette Square in the American Sector. The same streetcars that rumbled past the statue on Canal Street still rumble past its new home in Lafayette Square. There is also a major street in uptown New Orleans that bears Clay's name.

LAFAYETTE SQUARE

A place for protest in the nineteenth century, a place for relaxation in the twenty-first

Lafayette Square is the second-oldest park in New Orleans, dating to 1788. Originally called Place Gravier in 1824, it was renamed for Revolutionary War hero Gilbert du Motier, Marquis de La Fayette, after he visited here. Following the great fire in the Vieux Carré in 1788, Jackson Square became a tent city, and Lafayette Square became the gathering place for local meetings. It was the site of anti-Union demonstrations, mayoral inaugurations, and band concerts in the nineteenth century. The statue of Henry Clay was moved to the center of Lafayette Square from his place on the corner of Canal Street and St. Charles Avenue in 1900, shortly after this photo was taken.

Now firmly in place for over a century, Henry Clay surveys the increasing greenery of Lafayette Square. During the Depression in the 1930s, the Works Progress Administration executed both arts and construction projects here as part of their remit for job creation. The old oaks were damaged in Hurricane Katrina and some were lost, but the Lafayette Square Conservancy project has been active in restoring their natural beauty. Today Lafayette Square is still a park in the Warehouse/Arts District where one can take a lunch break or just relax on the benches and enjoy the shade. The square is host to "Wednesday at the Square," a free summer concert series featuring top local acts, and to the "Blues and Barbeque" festival in the fall.

NEW ORLEANS STREETCARS

The oldest streetcar service in the world

Even though the streetcar named Desire—which lent itself to the title of Tennessee Williams's play—was transformed into the less glamorous bus named Desire (inset), New Orleans retains an enduring affection for the streetcar, seen here in its mechanized form in the early 1900s on Canal Street. The city can claim to operate the oldest continuously operating street railway system in the world. That honor goes to the St. Charles Avenue line, which started as a horse-drawn service from 1835 and went electric in 1893. The Canal Street line, operated by the New Orleans Railroad Company, began service in 1861 and was electrified in 1894. Soon afterward, the Esplanade line was electrified. In 1901 the company extended both lines and connected them together in the Belt Line.

While the St. Charles Avenue line continued through the twentieth century, protected by preservationists who fought hard to give it landmark status, all other streetcar lines were converted to bus service. The distinctive electric streetcars were withdrawn from the late 1940s to the early 1960s when Canal Street lost its cars. Only Hurricane Katrina interrupted the St. Charles line. With the move toward greener technology in the late twentieth century, the streetcars made a comeback, first with a small Riverfront line and then, in 2004, a limited service on Canal Street (inset). The Regional Transit Authority, which is now responsible for the streetcars, has added further extensions on the St. Charles Avenue line despite the intervention of Katrina.

POYDRAS STREET / LOUISIANA SUPERDOME

A symbol of New Orleans's post-Katrina recovery

Left: Poydras Street near Claiborne was relatively undeveloped at the time of this 1920s photo. This part of town was beyond the areas of the business district, the Vieux Carré, and the American Sector. The river was still the focus of trade, even though the day of the steamboats had faded. In the 1920s, the land around Poydras Street was mostly owned by the railroads. The city originally grew up and down the Mississippi River from the Vieux Carré. But in later years it began to grow out from the river toward Lake Pontchartrain. In 1967 the architectural firm Curtis and Davis drew up plans for what would become the Louisiana Superdome. Work commenced on the site in 1971 and the stadium opened in 1975. The inset photo shows the damaged stadium being used as temporary accommodation in the wake of Hurricane Katrina.

Above: Of all the changes in New Orleans history, this area has to be one of the most dramatic. Where there was nothing but railroad yards now stands the Louisiana Superdome, home of the NFL's New Orleans Saints, and the New Orleans Arena, home of the NBA's New Orleans Hornets. Poydras Street, once a small dirt road, is now the main street of the New Orleans business district. In 2005 Hurricane Katrina wrecked the Superdome and damaged the New Orleans Arena. Both have been restored and are fully functional. The adjacent shopping center and Hyatt Hotel have never recovered. However, the Saints have taken over the office building in this complex and the area will be turned into a sports entertainment district in the coming years.

AUDUBON PLACE

A symbol of New Orleans's post-Katrina recovery

Left: Audubon Place was named after nearby Audubon Park and sits on the lake side of St. Charles, the grand American residential avenue of New Orleans. Audubon had one of the very few private streets in the city. The imposing Richardson Romanesque gates designed by architect Thomas Sully fit in perfectly with nearby Tulane University, which was also designed using this distinctive architectural style. In fact, the president of Tulane University lives in a university-owned mansion close to the entrance to Audubon Place.

Above: Audubon Place is now part of the University District. Along with Tulane University, there is also Loyola University, which absorbed the nearby Saint Mary's Dominican College, a liberal arts college for women, in 1984. Audubon remains an upmarket residential community. During the flooding brought on by Hurricane Katrina in 2005, it remained dry thanks to its position above sea level. However, with homes averaging $5 million, security personnel were helicoptered in to keep any unwelcome visitors out.

TULANE UNIVERSITY, NEW ORLEANS, LA.

TULANE UNIVERSITY

Designed in the grand Richardson Romanesque style

Left: This is a photo of Tulane University in 1903. Tulane University started life in 1834 as the brainchild of seven young doctors, and was established as the Medical College of Louisiana in 1837. In 1882 Paul Tulane, a prosperous local merchant, deeded real estate for the foundation of an institution of "a higher grade of learning." A New Jersey native, Tulane had made his fortune in New Orleans and wanted to give back some of it to his adopted city. In 1884 the state reorganized the institution and it became a private university with the name Tulane in gratitude for the benefactor's donation. In 1886 the H. Sophie Newcomb Memorial College was established for women as part of the university. The main campus, set on St. Charles Avenue directly across from Audubon Park, is a beautiful area filled with fine architecture and landscaping.

Above: Today Tulane University has over 11,000 students from all fifty states and about eighty foreign countries. The main campus has over 110 acres with a school of medicine, and a school of public health and tropical medicine. In downtown New Orleans, Tulane runs a hospital and clinic and is the largest private employer in the city. In 2005 the university suffered damage as a result of Hurricane Katrina and for the first time since the Civil War was forced to close for a semester. In 2006 Tulane reorganized and emerged from the effects of the storm with 93 percent of its students returning. Tulane continues to grow and maintains its high position among fine American universities.

BAYOU ST. JOHN

No longer a shortcut to the Gulf of Mexico

Left: Bayou St. John was originally the Choupithatcha waterway that the local Native Americans showed to French explorers Iberville and Bienville. The bayou was a shorter and safer route from the Mississippi River to the Gulf of Mexico (via Lake Pontchartrain) than the treacherous voyage the Frenchmen had originally made up the mouth of the Mississippi River. A deciding factor in the location of New Orleans, it was originally much longer and a major shipping route. In 1803 a canal was dredged from the bayou to Basin Street, and another canal, built in 1838, became a primary commercial route. This photo was taken in 1902 when the bayou was still a major waterway. A section of the bayou that flowed into the old Basin and Carondelet canals was drained by the government, and has not been fully navigable since the 1930s. Bayou St. John runs in part along Esplanade Avenue, across from City Park.

Above: Bayou St. John is located in what is now termed the Mid-City, or Faubourg St. John area, and is dotted with historic homes, including the Pitot House built in 1799. The area is considered prime real estate for large and elegant homes. It is a favorite site for strolling, canoeing, bicycling, and the like. At different parts, the bayou is home to the Holy Rosary Catholic Church and the Holy Trinity Greek Orthodox Church. A relatively new music event, the "Bayou Boogaloo," is held on the bayou in the spring. The bayou still meanders from Lake Pontchartrain deep into the city of New Orleans, much as it did when Bienville founded the city. It is no longer used for commerce, but is a source of pleasurable recreation for the inhabitants of New Orleans.

This home was built on the shore of Bayou St. John in 1799 by Don Bartolome Bosque and was originally used as a summer cottage. At the time it was built, this area was open country and was a welcome retreat from the city, with its view of the bayou and cool breezes. This 1964 photo shows the house's original location at 1370 Moss Street. The Pitot House is named for the home's fourth owner, James Pitot, the first mayor of New Orleans, who lived in the house from 1810 to 1819.

MICHEL PITOT HOUSE

A historic house that was moved two blocks to escape the wrecking ball

In the late 1960s, the Pitot House was moved to 1440 Moss Street to avoid demolition. Twentieth-century additions were removed and the house was restored to the way it looked at the time Pitot lived there. The house is now a museum that is also open to the public for special events. The house has been furnished with Louisianan and American antiques that date from the early 1800s. Although the home is completely furnished with antiques of the period, the only original piece to the home is a portrait of Pitot's daughter, Sophie Gabrielle. The colonial museum tells the story of what life was like along Bayou St. John for the early settlers of New Orleans. The Louisiana Landmarks Society uses the house as its headquarters, opens it for tours, and rents out the lawn and gardens for special events.

PERISTYLE CITY PARK

A place to revel in the beauty of ancient live oak trees

Left: City Park is 1,500 acres of live oak trees, wandering bayous, a sculpture garden, the New Orleans Museum of Art, and the site of many duels in days gone by. It contains the largest stand of live oak trees in the world, and some trees are over 600 years old. Many buildings in the park are landmarks, and the Peristyle is no exception. The Peristyle, built in 1907 as a dance pavilion, is one of the oldest structures. This photo taken shortly after it was built in 1907 shows the Peristyle's neoclassical design, Ionic columns, and stone lions. It was once the perfect place for dancing or watching a performance of Shakespeare.

Above: Not much dancing goes on in the Peristyle today. However, it remains a favorite picnic spot for families and a place to daydream about simpler times. Recently, the Louisiana Philharmonic Orchestra has begun a tradition of performing free concerts in the Peristyle in spring. City Park is currently undergoing a much-needed restoration after being damaged by Hurricane Katrina. Some of the live oaks were lost, and many were damaged. Because the park gets no funding from the City of New Orleans, it depends on revenues collected and private donations, so the progress is slow but steady.

WADING POOL

Enjoyed by numerous children over the generations

Above: In 1914 Sara Lavinia Hyams donated this wading pool to the children of New Orleans. It is shown here in the summer of 1929, with children enjoying an afternoon in City Park by cooling off in the pool. Generations of children have lazed away many afternoons in this wading pool in much the same way. City Park sits on the site of the old Allard Plantation facing Bayou St. John. Climbing the massive live oak trees, fishing in the lagoons and bayous, and enjoying the antique carousel were favorite pastimes of the children of New Orleans in the 1920s. The wading pool was close to a miniature train that took riders all through the park.

Right: Today the pool is enclosed in the Carousel Gardens Amusement Park. The amusement park also includes an antique wooden carousel featuring the masterwork of famed carousel carvers Charles Looff and Charles Carmel. The amusement park also has several other fun rides, including the Lady Bug, a miniature roller-coaster that winds through huge live oak trees. The old trees still get climbed on and fish are pulled out of the lagoons and bayous on a regular basis. Families still picnic under the oaks and kids still cool off in the wading pool.

GIVEN TO THE LITTLE CHILDREN
OF NEW ORLEANS
BY
SARA LAVINIA HYAMS
·MCMXIV·

MONKEY HILL

Teaching the children of New Orleans what a hill looked like

Left: Located in the Audubon Zoo, Monkey Hill was created during the Depression as part of a Work Projects Administration initiative. Local lore has it that the hill was made to show the nature of a hill to New Orleans children who were accustomed only to flat land. It was long believed to be the highest point in New Orleans, a little over twenty-five feet high. It has always been a favorite destination at the zoo, and as seen in this photo from 1966, was bare of any adornment save the trails left by climbing children who found the hill to be exotic. One tradition among the children of New Orleans was to ski down Monkey Hill. Once a year, shaved ice was spread over the hill for this purpose.

Above: Monkey Hill is no longer considered the top peak, as another hill in City Park is about two feet higher. However, when the zoo was completely renovated in the 1980s, the Audubon Institute landscaped the hill, adorning it with streams, trees, and animal sculptures. Although they are generally more traveled than their grandparents and most have seen real mountains, local children are still fascinated with their own new and improved Monkey Hill. The stream cascading down the hill provides a great place to splash and get a little wet on hot summer afternoons. At the top of the hill are bronze sculptures of a lioness and her cubs.

FAIR GROUNDS RACETRACK

The grandstand for America's oldest racetrack is hoping that it's third time lucky

Horse racing has been a part of New Orleans since the 1850s. The original track at Fair Grounds on Gentilly Road was the Union Race Track, built in 1852, thus making it the oldest site in the United States still in operation as a racetrack. In 1872 the Louisiana Jockey Club was formed and ran their first race card at the Fair Grounds. In 1894 the Crescent City Jockey Club inaugurated a race known as the Crescent City Derby. Since the 1870s, with the exception of the years between 1908 and 1915, when horse racing was banned in New Orleans, great thoroughbreds have run the course at the Fair Grounds. This photo shows the course and grandstand as it appeared in 1906.

A tragic fire destroyed the grandstand in 1919, but the racing continued and the grandstand was rebuilt. The "new" grandstand burned in 1993, and was again rebuilt. The Fair Grounds was purchased by Churchill Downs in 2004 and has grown in prestige and acclaim. Thanksgiving Day is opening day at the Fair Grounds, and that has become a New Orleans tradition. Since 1972 the site has been known for something even bigger than horse racing. The New Orleans Jazz and Heritage Festival has been held in the infield of the racetrack every year in April and May, bringing hundreds of thousands of people into the Fair Grounds to taste the music, food, and culture of New Orleans.

05766 LIFE BOAT PRACTICE, WEST END, NEW ORLEANS.

DETROIT PHOTOGRAPHIC CO.

WEST END AT LAKE PONTCHARTRAIN

Formerly a navigational thoroughfare, it soon became a place for recreational boating

Left: This is West End Park on Lake Pontchartrain in 1901, during a lifeboat drill to recover a man who has fallen overboard. In the mid-1800s West End Park was home to fishermen, crabbers, hunters, and trappers. Later this spot became a magnet for recreational boaters; the Southern Yacht Club, which can trace its roots to 1849, also established itself here. Visible at the top of the photograph is their grand club building, completed in 1899. In 1870 "Smoky Mary," the city's passenger train, began transporting citizens to the area when restaurants and jazz clubs sprang up at West End Park and Milneburg.

Above: Lake Pontchartrain is still New Orleans's water playground, though it is no longer used as a shipping canal for a shorter route to New Orleans. It's a large, shallow lake perfect for sailing or boating of any kind. The 1899 clubhouse of the Southern Yacht Club had deteriorated so much by 1949 that it had to be replaced. The structure was renovated in the 1960s, but was destroyed by Hurricane Katrina in 2005. Since then, it has been rebuilt and restaurants again serve up fresh seafood to hungry boaters. Recent efforts to clean up the lake, which became polluted in the 1960s, have been successful and it is again open to swimmers on the south shore.

METAIRIE CEMETERY

The elegant resting place for people from all walks of life

Left: New Orleans is known for its cemeteries, called "cities of the dead." The tradition of aboveground burials in New Orleans can be traced to the city's French and Spanish heritage. In 1838 the land here was used as a racetrack and hosted the famous 1854 Lexington-Lecomte race billed as "the North against the South." During the Civil War the track was used as a training ground for Confederate soldiers. After the war was over, it went bankrupt and was turned into a cemetery by Charles T. Howard who had been refused membership in the Jockey Club. The layout of the tombs and roads on Metairie Cemetery's oval plan make it evident that this once was a racetrack. This photo, circa 1930, shows a street lined with typical aboveground tombs.

Above: Little has changed over time, although the tombs do suffer from the ravages of hurricane-force winds. The streets are all named and avenues are in alphabetical order, but they don't look much different now. The roads in this "city of the dead" are lined with beautiful oak trees and the tombs are ornate and well kept. Rustic iron work fences surround many of the sun-bleached tombs, and fine examples of funereal art adorn them. It is a tradition in New Orleans to spend November 1, the Feast of All Saints, cleaning and repairing family graves. Many famous people are buried in Metairie including New Orleans district attorney Jim Garrison, former Byrds guitarist Gram Parsons, General P. G. T. Beauregard, World War II boat pioneer Andrew Higgins, jazz trumpeter Al Hirt, and baseball star Mel Ott. Legendary Storyville madame Josie Arlington has a grand tomb as well.

ARMY OF THE TENNESSEE MEMORIAL

The cornerstone of the Metairie Cemetery

Left: This monument to the Louisiana Division of the Tennessee Army in the Civil War is one of the most famous tombs in the Metairie Cemetery. This photo, circa 1900, shows the monument that holds forty-eight vaults. Atop the memorial is an 1877 equestrian statue of General Albert Sidney Johnston. Before the emergence of Robert E. Lee, Jefferson Davis considered Johnston the finest officer in the Confederate army. Johnston was killed at the Battle of Shiloh in 1862 and was the highest-ranking officer of either side killed in the conflict. He was interred here temporarily until his body could be returned home to Austin, Texas. On one side of the monument stands a life-size statue of a Confederate officer giving a roll call of those killed in the Civil War. Over the tomb is a vine-covered mound. At the back of the tomb is a marble tablet with a list of every battle in which the Army of Tennessee fought.

Above: Perhaps the most notable aspect of this photo is how little has changed over the years. General Johnston still rides his faithful horse Fire-eater above the monument while holding his binoculars. The Louisiana soldier—believed to be modeled on Sergeant William Brunet of the Louisiana Guard Battery—still holds the roll of the dead as if about to read the names aloud. Like Johnston, Jefferson Davis was buried here for a short while before being moved to Hollywood Cemetery in Richmond, Virginia. The only thing that is really changed is the traffic on the interstate highway directly behind the monument, which was built in the 1960s. The monument, funded by the surviving Louisiana soldiers of the Army of Tennessee and dedicated on April 6, 1877, is the cornerstone of the Metairie Cemetery.

BANKS OF THE MISSISSIPPI RIVER

Waiting to receive travelers from Baton Rouge, Natchez, Cairo, and St. Louis

Left: This early 1860s photograph shows how busy New Orleans had become in the years just prior to the Civil War. The impact of the conflict, which brought traffic on the river to a virtual halt, and the impact of railroad expansion, brought about a dramatic decline. The young Samuel Clemens (later to change his name to Mark Twain) had trained as a steamboat pilot on the Mississippi River from St. Louis down to New Orleans, backward and forward in an exhausting apprenticeship. On his return to the river in 1882 to make notes for his book *Life on the Mississippi,* he was shocked at the number of steamboats he found in New Orleans. "The vast reach of plank wharves remained unchanged, and there were as many ships as ever: but the long array of steamboats had vanished; not altogether, of course, but not much of it was left."

Above: Mark Twain would still recognize many parts of New Orleans, but the passing of the steamboats and the lost craft of piloting a boat through treacherous shoals and endlessly shifting mudbanks would have brought him a profound sadness. Access to the river and the steamboats that still operate on the great old river is easy. The Moonwalk, named for New Orleans mayor Maurice "Moon" Landrieu, runs from the Canal Street Wharf downriver to the edge of the French Quarter. Steps go down from the Moonwalk to the river's edge, making the "Big Muddy" available to all. This part of the river is no longer about commerce and shipping. It's about enjoyment and appreciation of the power and beauty of America's greatest river.

OYSTER LUGGERS AT THE LEVEE

New Orleans has long enjoyed a love affair with the Louisiana oyster

Left: This photo shows oyster luggers landing on the riverfront between St. Phillip and Hospital (now Governor Nicholls) streets in the 1890s. In the nineteenth century, oyster luggers, specially designed boats with open deck space to accommodate oyster storage, would dock and sell their catch to a welcoming crowd. The oyster fishermen used hang tongs to harvest the oysters from the riverbed. The luggers had plenty of walking space along the sides and stern to allow for the operation of these tongs. Oystermen would signal their arrival at the wharves by blowing on conch shells. Oyster fishing was hard work done by the young and hardy who could operate the tongs and lift the large sacks of oysters after they were harvested from the beds.

Above: Oyster fishermen would lease oyster reefs or water bottoms from their local parishes, on which they had the rights to harvest the shellfish. These rights were transferred to the State of Louisiana in 1902. Back then, they would sell oysters for around $3 to $4 a barrel. Today oysters are harvested year-round using the "dredge" method invented in 1905, but they are no longer landed on the levee. New Orleans has always had a love affair with oysters. They are served raw in the half shell, charbroiled, cooked as oysters Rockefeller, oysters Bienville, in soup, as dressing for Thanksgiving turkeys, fried on French bread, and just about any other way you can come up with.

HIGGINS BOATYARD

One of the unsung heroes of World War II

Left: Andrew Higgins designed the landing craft, vehicle, personnel (LCVP) that were used on the beaches of Normandy on D-Day. The boats were designed and tested in New Orleans. Higgins had several shipyards in New Orleans during the 1940s. One of them was in a swampy area in the eastern part, as seen in this 1942 photo. Lake Pontchartrain and the Industrial Canal also played a big part in Higgins's success. It was along these waterways that Higgins tested his new design. General Dwight D. Eisenhower said: "If Higgins had not designed and built those LCVPs, we never could have landed over an open beach. The whole strategy of the war would have been different."

Above: After the war, demand for Higgins's landing craft and fast patrol vessels dwindled. His shipyards no longer exist in New Orleans, although one part of his company still makes yachts in the city. The swampy area where Higgins made and tested his boats is now occupied by the NASA Michaud Assembly Facility (inset). Michaud is one of the largest employers in Louisiana with over 4,000 employees. On its 832 acres, Michaud has the capacity to manufacture large aerospace structures such as external fuel tanks. Higgins is still remembered in New Orleans; there is a street named after him that leads from Lee Circle and passes in front of the National World War II Museum. Just inside the front entrance of that museum is the LCVP that General Eisenhower praised so much.

BOURBON STREET

The most famous street in New Orleans and the center of many celebrations

Contrary to popular belief, Bourbon Street was not named for the alcoholic beverage. It was named—like many of the streets in the Vieux Carré—for one of the royal houses of France, the house of Bourbon, which was the ruling house of France at the time New Orleans was planned. The original name of this street was Rue Bourbon. When the Americans took over in 1803, all "Rues" were changed to "Streets." In the early twentieth century, jazz clubs and bawdy vaudeville theaters sprang up along Bourbon Street. By the 1940s, Bourbon Street added neon lights and nightclubs featuring burlesque shows, as shown in this 1946 photo. Its reputation was sealed.

Bourbon Street is the most famous street in the French Quarter, if not in all of New Orleans. Street parties for Mardi Gras, the Jazz Fest, the French Quarter Festival, the Super Bowl, the Sugar Bowl, or just because it's Tuesday are well known around the world. Bourbon Street has more than just bars and nightclubs; it also has fine restaurants and hotels. Yet, it's still only one street in one section of one great city.